Photography by Guido Karp

Management by Blitz. Another BIG product

Written by Belinda Jones
Designed by Jason Bazini

Published by
Grandreams Limited
435-437 Edgware Road, Little Venice, London, W2 1TH

Printed in Belgium

• Grandreams - For the children of the world •
• London - New York - Sydney - Auckland - Bath •

CONTENTS

PETER'S MESSAGE

Hi! This is a message to my girl - whoever you are - reading this annual right now!

Actually it's a message to all the guys and mums and dads out there too! Welcome to my official annual! This is a chance for you to get to know me a little bit better - within these pages you'll find out everything from my favourite song to kiss to, to how many sit-ups I do a day and why I'd be a koala if I could be any animal There's also a look behind-the-scenes of my videos and some revealing observations from my birth chart - just how did they know I like telling jokes in funny accents!?

This has been an amazing year for me - being accepted for my music as well as my image - and I really do appreciate the fact that you have made it happen for me! You are always in my thoughts and I never forget that it is your support that is helping me make all my dreams come true - I love ya for it

I'm really looking forward to the year ahead and I hope you are too! Let's kick it

I'm single and I'm looking for my dream girl but I still feel I've been lucky in love. It's a very important part of my life - love fills that little gap inside you that can sometimes seem like a big gap. It warms you and it's great to know someone is thinking of you. You can buy anything but you can't buy love - that's why they say money can't buy you happiness, unless you've got love you're not truly happy. At least that's the way it seems - being in love makes you content so I am always striving for that.

Of course it's not all hearts and flowers and happiness! The worst thing about being in love for me is that when that person's not around it can play on my mind and stop me doing other things

and I can make myself miserable. But then it really doesn't take much to make me happy again - sometimes just a phone call means a lot. You can be in that mood where everything gets you down and one phone call can pick you up and put that smile back on your face!

I'd say the best thing about being in a relationship with me is that I love giving - I'm a giver in all areas. I'm always conscious of how the other person is feeling and hoping that they are enjoying themselves, but that can be a bad thing because they end up saying, 'Would you stop worrying!' And I always want to give 100% but I'm away such a lot that I can't do that. The downside to dating me is that when I fall for someone I fall

MR LOVERMAN

Peter opens his heart to you...

deep and I get a bit too close and involved and I guess I expect a lot in return. I guess I'm an all or nothing kind of person!

As I say, I am looking to meet someone special and what tends to engage me is the way the girl uses her eyes - you can always tell what someone is thinking from the little expressions they make with their eyes and movements with their lips and their tongue, so I tend to stand back and observe for a while. Sometimes instinct tells you to go up and say, 'Why don't we stop just looking at each other and do something about it?' but I can get shy around someone I

like. Occasionally I'll be blunt and say something like, 'Are you thinking what I'm thinking?' But only if I'm certain she's giving me that look!

My idea of a perfect date would be to take a girl for dinner at a French restaurant where we can enjoy some red wine. Afterwards I might suggest going for a walk, or going to see a movie or just going back to my place and listen to some music. Luther Vandross and candles create a lovely mood!

Anyway, if my dream girl is out there reading this, I just want her to know I'm looking forward to meeting her!'

HANDWRITING ANALYSIS

To the Readers of The Official Peter Andre Annual: I just wanna say — "This One's from Me to you."

Let's whip out the magnifying glass and get to grips with some graphology to see if we can discover Peter Andre's true nature from his handwriting!

All My Love From

SCRIPT SIZE - The handwriting is normal in size - neither itsy bitsy small or flamboyantly big. This simply means he is well-balanced mentally and socially.

As you will see from his letter 'f' in the word 'Official' the upper zone (above the horizontal stroke) is larger. This area represents the intellect, ambition, spiritual awareness and creative talent and shows Peter to be imaginative, idealistic and enthusiastic. It can also mean the writer is extravagant, power-seeking and daydreaming!

With the 'y' in 'say' and 'you' the lower zone is emphasized and this shows a need for a physically active life. The loop in the 'y' in 'say' shows the writer is preoccupied with dreams and has a caring attitude, strong physical desires and sensual feelings.

SLANT - The words: 'To The Readers of The Official Peter' have a slight rightward slant showing 'forward looking'. This is basically an extrovert trait belonging to someone who can be impatient and excitable but also sympathetic and relaxed. This writer would rather work in a group than by himself and has a willingness to share experiences with others.

The majority of his writing is upright. This means the head rules the heart. The upright slant writer is cool, calm, collected, independent and prefers order. (Peter is, however, by his own admission disorganized and excitable.)

To the Readers of The Official Peter Andre Annual:

I just wanna say — "This One's from Me to you."

Because there is 'mixed slant' this means the writer is versatile in his thinking but also changeable and moods can be unpredictable.

WIDTH - looking at the letter 'n' in 'Annual' and 'wanna' we see a wide script. This shows the writer to be friendly, expressive and generous but maybe a little hasty!

CONNECTION - not all the letters are 'joined up' - see 'just' and the first three letters of 'Readers'. This shows the writer to be adaptable, full of ideas and intuitive.

FORM - This is basically a plain script meaning the writer is purposeful with a clear thinking ability and a mature attitude. However it can also mean the person is unpunctual and indecisive.

PEN STROKE - This thick stroke is known as 'pastose' and is favoured by those who are dominated by their senses! In fact they have a heightened sense of touch, smell, taste and vision and have a developed sense of beauty. They need warm bodily contact and are tactile by nature!

PRESSURE - The reasonably heavy pressure indicates these traits: strong willpower, seeking success, energetic. But this writer can overstretch himself in his determination to get where he wants to be but he won't quit until he achieves his aims.

SPACING - The writer has quite large gaps between each word and wide spacing between the lines and that isolated look of the words indicates the writer may suffer from loneliness - but would not admit it to anyone. What they really want is an intimate, emotional personal involvement.

REGULARITY - The script is somewhat irregular and changeable and this indicates the writer is open-minded, spontaneous and has many interests. But it can also mean the writer is easily influenced and distracted.

PERSONAL PRONOUN - That's 'I' to us normal folk! This is about how you view yourself and the writer's script is plain and upright and in keeping with the size of the rest of the script which indicates moderate self-confidence and a practical, objective side.

CAPITALS - Plain large capitals hint at an ambitious, and possibly creative person who desires recognition for his efforts - the showbiz personality type. (Oh yes!)

RESULT: Spookily spot-on!

VIDEO DIARIES

TURN IT UP

The scene: Stark loft with Peter and five dancers shaking their thang, turntables spinning and a girl rapping into the freezer compartment of a fridge - cool!

Peter says: This was the first video I shot in Britain. We invited extras to come along for this video and we were expecting to have 200-300 turn up, but on the day only about 10 people arrived! And we were lucky to have them because one of our dancers had dragged them there! We told the camera guy we wanted it to look crammed and somehow he managed to give that impression and it turned out alright!

SIX OF THE BES

ONLY ONE

The scene: Swinging hammocks, pool-side bikini babes, rewound dives, lanterns and torches lighting the night scenes and best of all, Peter in a vest displaying th most awesome biceps.

Peter says: We trauled all the way to the other side of the world - literally - for this video! The idea was to catch the sun but when we got to Australia it rainec practically the whole time! We ended up doing most of the filming at night but still has that 'summer love' feel to it and for some reason it ended up being one of the most fun videos to make!

MYSTERIOUS GIRL

The scene: Lush, tropical, enticing - and the scenery wasn't bad either! Peter Andre and Bubbla Ranxs wade through idyllic turquoise waters of a lagoon and hang with the locals of Phi Phi Island.

Peter says: The 'mysterious girl' was chosen for me and when I got there it turned out to be this girl called Champagne that I used to date! I was supposed to have a couple of days to recover from the long flight to Thailand but I didn't even get a chance to work-out before we started shooting literally an hour after I got off the plane! We did the waterfall scene first and thankfully the light was so beautiful it worked out. Some of the James Bond movies were filmed on this island and it's probably one of my favourite places in the world!

This was the first video I co-edited and now I always have a hand in choosing the shots and putting the thing together.

I FEEL YOU

The scene: As classy and smooth as coffee and cream, this video has Peter pacing the wooden floorboards of his spacious home (shown like the section of a doll's house so you can peer into more than one room) lamenting a loss of love. It's snowing and he's all wrapped up in a snuggly jumper and then unwrapped as he remembers their steamy sensuality...

Peter says: Well, well, well! This is probably one of the most interesting video shoots because I got my wish of making contact with the girl in the video! Charlene and I did a bit more than make contact and some people considered the intimate scenes too provocative and there was a lot of editing to be done!

FLAVA

The scene: A *Baywatch* lifeguard towering on Venice Beach, Peter slicing through the sand in his electric blue jeep, a technicolour gang whooping it up in the scorching sunshine and then hanging pool-side under a streaky pink sunset.

Peter says: I have mixed memories of this shoot because I did get seriously ill for five days as the result of dehydration, being out in the midday sun and then eating one piece of dodgy fish! It's a lesson to always keep drinking water. Even though I was pretty wiped out, I'm still pleased with the result. We found this amazing graffitti area that was the perfect backdrop and I didn't mind at all that one of the dancers - Brandy - looked exactly like Halle Berry! There was also this great guy called No Bones who can just slam his body down onto concrete and fold his knees up by his head - he's like a contortionist and a brilliant dancer, I'm hoping to work with him again sometime in the future.

ATURAL

scene: Aircraft hangars pulsating with party people in dungarees, spiral-haired s in yellow anoraks and black kneepads giving it their all on the wet tarmac, owing white shirts and the main man standing on the wing of a plane. Come with me...

er says: This is the second video we shot in LA - I love that place, it has such zing energy and a great atmosphere. We had to get up horribly early to get yellow and blue sunrise but it was worth it! The dancers did a superb job - when they were being blasted with hose pipes - and the whole shoot was a

IF I WAS...

AN ANIMAL I'd be a koala, so I could just chill out and eat leaves all day!

A MOVIE I'd be Scarface with Al Pacino.

A COLOUR I'd be aqua blue because I like calming things and that's a calming colour!

AN EMOTION I'd be a combination of happy and sensual!

A COUNTRY I'd be America because it's the land of opportunity!

A SMELL I'd be an attractive one I hope! Something tropical!

AN ITEM OF CLOTHING I'd be a pair of shades!

A MONTH OF THE YEAR I'd be June because it's a sunny, happy month

A KISS I'd be a luscious one!

A CAR I'd be a Lamborghini Countach

I AM...

Peter, please highlight the words that you feel best describe your personality...

SHY RESERVED CAUTIOUS NERVOUS FRETFUL QUIET DREAMER

AMBITIOUS DETERMINED FOCUSED SINCERE CONSIDERATE

THOUGHTFUL CALM ENERGETIC LETHARGIC CONFUSED

OPTIMISTIC PESSIMISTIC CYNICAL UNSURE HAPPY CONTENT

PASSIONATE SPONTANEOUS TEMPERAMENTAL CONFIDENT

ARROGANT SELF-CONSCIOUS SELFISH GENEROUS SENSITIVE

FUNNY (sometimes - well I laugh anyway!) FORGETFUL DISORGANISED

METHODICAL WARM INTROVERT EXTROVERT EXCITABLE JEALOUS

POSSESSIVE OBSESSIVE SUSPICIOUS SARCASTIC POLITE (I hope!)

Photography by Guido Karp

EASY-GOING PERFECTIONIST INTENSE PROUD PLAYFUL

LOVING IMAGINATIVE QUIRKY CHEEKY LIVELY ANIMATED

SERIOUS SEDUCTIVE WHOLESOME BOLD IDEALISTIC GENTLE

I WISH I WAS MORE... SEDUCTIVE

I WISH I WAS LESS... DISORGANIZED

MALE OX TRAITS THAT APPLY TO PETER

Hard-working, conscientious and industrious. It is said he may spend long hours slogging away at the sort of tasks that would send less patient types doolally!

There's a big difference between the image the Ox presents to the world at large and the impression the folk at home get!

In a group situation he won't be the loudest. He may even be shy in the company of strangers or those he is unsure of.

He is good at listening to someone else's viewpoint.

Beneath that 'tough hide' the Ox has a lot of love to offer - he is deeply affectionate, sensual and able to express his most heartfelt emotions. (Not that he has a tough hide in the first place!)

The Ox loves to lie for hours - alone or not - in a hot bath.

The Ox enjoys cooking a meal but a quiet evening at home can turn into something more. When the Ox is free from inhibition he can take some keeping up with!

The Ox is highly charged sexually and is as boisterous in the bedroom as he is quiet elsewhere!

Apparently the Ox is capable of 'physical feats that many others would find impossible to emulate!'

The Ox individual feels everything with an intensity few experience.

Once you have won the heart of the Ox you'd be hard pushed to find a more ardent or sincere lover.
TRAITS THAT DON'T APPLY The Ox is neat and methodical. (*No way José!*)

he Ox is not naturally talkative.

or a more specific reading, we look at the combination of Ox with his ement WATER -

VATER OX - TRAITS THAT APPLY

e Water Ox is the ultimate gentle and caring character in the Chinese -diac. This can be tricky to live with because the standards are so darn gh, but his love of family and home is second to none. He is potentially e most romantic and poetic person you could imagine.

HOROSCOPE

eter Andre was born in 1973 on 27th ebruary which means his element is VATER and his sign is the OX.

RAITS THAT DON'T APPLY

ow and steady, predictable, plodding, follower of routines... ot the most entertaining person around'! We don't think so!

X IN LOVE

e OX is best suited to a relationship with a TIGER, RABBIT or PIG

LUCKY

NUMBERS

20 significant numbers
for Peter Andre...

24-7 In *Natural* Peter sings: 'I wanna get with you, 24-7 baby'. That means 24 hours a day, 7 days a week!

5 This is the age Peter had his first kiss - he went out with the girl in questio Miranda, for four years

This is the house number Peter lived at in Harrow - 1 Sudbury Road

9 This was Peter's age when he first moved to Australia

50 This is the number of Australian cents Peter's school charged pupils to see lunch-time performances

92 This is the mark out of 100 that Peter received for his performance of Bobb Brown's *Don't Be Cruel* on the Australian talent show *New Faces*

7 This is the age Peter was when he signed his record contract with Mushroo

300 This is the number of people who bought tickets to Peter's first concert in the Gold Coast

3 This is the age Peter started doing sit-ups at the gym

300 This is the number of sit-ups Peter does a day

30 This is the number of minutes Peter does a vocal warm-up for before a sho

Photography by Guido Karp

90   This is the number of minutes Peter performed on stage for the *Natural Tour*

4   This is the number of brothers Peter has. He also has one sister - Debbie

72   This is the chart position Peter's first single *Drive Me Crazy* went to in Oz

3,000   This is the number of copies *Drive Me Crazy* sold in Australia

750,000 This is the number of copies *Mysterious Girl* sold in the UK - double platinum

8,000   This is the number of members in the Peter Andre Fan Club. As for the database of fans held by the record company - that's a whopping 350,000!

5   This is the number of awards that Peter won at the Australian Music Awards in 1993, including Best Selling Single of the Year for *Gimme Little Sign*

27   This is the day of the month Peter was born - 27th February 1973.

100   This is how much he appreciates his fans - 100%!

EITHER/OR

Choose one of the following pairs!

CAT OR DOG? Puppy - because they are loved and respected but never crossed!

Thai or Indian takeaway? Thai is my absolute favourite because it has a freshness about it.

Whitney Housten or Toni Braxton? Whitney Housten vocally, Toni Braxton all other reasons!

Los Angeles or New York? Los Angeles because it seems a happy place - I love it. I'm spending about three months of this year in LA writing new material and getting inspired!

Party all night or couch potato? Party all night on the couch!

Bath or shower? Depends on my mood, mmm, let's go for bath! I like to take my time.

Jean-Claude Van Damme or Bruce Lee? Physique of Van Damme, speed of Bruce Lee. They are both my heroes.

Sea or swimming pool? For swimming I'd choose the pool because you're in control of it rather than it being in control of you.

Kissing or hugging? Either - I'm not fussy!

Calvin Klein or Armani? Armani because it has a class to it.

Single or 'coupled'? This stage of my life, definitely single!

Ballad or dance track? People need to move and be happy so I'll go for dance track!

Eddie Murphy or Wil Smith? Eddie - he's richer! Seriously, I'd pick him because he's such a versatile actor and quite underrated in my opinion!

Beavis & Butthead or The Simpsons? *Simpsons* just because they make me smile!

Neighbours or Home & Away? I know more people in *Home & Away* so it has to be that!

Sunset or sunrise? Depends on who I'm with! Both are beautiful scenes to share.

Video or cinema? I love the movies, man! One day I'd like to have a screening room in my house with big speakers, big screen, the works! I'd choose cinema but ideally in my own home!!

Salt or sweet popcorn? Has to be mixed! Mixed is the best. Just when you've had enough of the salt it turns beautifully sweet!

Pierced or natural bellybutton (on a girl)? Natural is always better but piercing is quite a turn-on!

Big jumpers or tight tops? Big jumpers in the winter, tight tops in the summer - as long as they are v-necks - they are cool!

Blondes or brunettes? In theory I go for dark, exotic girls but I've also dated blonde girls and I didn't mind a bit!

Home cooking or eating out? I love cooking exotic Creole foods like chicken with coconut milk but I'm really an Italian at heart! As a treat I guess I'd choose eating out because I love going to French restaurants and enjoying a bottle of red wine with my meal, and of course some lovely company!

Britain or Australia? It has always been my dream to perform on my home territory and Britain is the musical capital of the world so I'll go for the UK!

Dark or milk chocolate? Ahh milk! British milk chocolate - I like Cadbury's because it's rich.

Champagne or fizzy water? Champagne, of course!

Wakey Wakey!

I'm not a morning person at all. Getting up is just the worst! My brothers (Danny & Chris) and I are always really quiet until the day gets going. About half way through the day I'm bright and happy and this lasts until about 6pm, then I'll be tired for a couple of hours. About 8pm I get a whole new feeling and I can stay awake right through the night!

Sleepyhead

I find it difficult to fall asleep unless I'm really exhausted because I have so much on my mind. I lie down and try to imagine that absolutely everything surrounding me is white and before I know it, I'm asleep.

Bedroom bliss

I've got black satin sheets - it's just the best feeling to get into bed after I've had a shower.

Sweet Dreams

I'm not aware of dreaming that much although I did have a recurring dream when I was younger - it had a kind of Mafia theme to it but instead of people there was a parade of thumbs - a big thumb leading the way for lots of baby thumbs. There was confetti in the air and I was watching them from across the road in a tree. I don't know what it means but it used to freak me out!

IN BED WITH PETER ANDRE

Big Breakfast?

Actually, no! I don't eat breakfast! But I did spend a week knocking on people's doors as a guest presenter on the TV show the *Big Breakfast*! It was hilarious - I couldn't believe how nice people were about having a film crew turn up uninvited at their homes!

Sleeping position

Twisted! It's very hard to describe my sleeping position - I lie with my arms across my chest, on my stomach but half on one side and a quarter in the middle - I can't explain!

Night music

In bed I like to unwind by listening to soul voices like Anita Baker and Luther Vandross.

Forty winks

When we were first promoting in Britain I was averaging about two hours sleep a night because we'd be in the studio all day and then doing appearances in clubs around the country in the evening. Some days I just went through 24 hours without stopping! It was crazy. I can cope on just a few hours because I am very motivated about what I am getting up for but if I get a chance to catch up on sleep anywhere - like the tour bus - I will!

ZZZZZ Do I snore? I don't know - if I do, it's not loud enough to wake myself up!

MY PERFECT SONG TO...

CRY TO... *Run To You* by Whitney Housten

KISS TO... *Perfect Love Affair* by Anita Baker

GET FRISKY TO... *Sexual Healing* by Marvin Gaye

BE ALONE WITH... *Just Once* by James Inghram

WAKE UP TO... *Ribbon in the Sky* by Stevie Wonder

GO TO SLEEP TO... *Every Time I Close My Eyes* by Babyface

DANCE TO... any James Brown track!

DRIVE TO... *Smooth Operator* by Sade

SING ALONG TO... *Secret Garden* by Quincey Jones

LIFT YOUR SPIRITS... *One Love* by Bob Marley

PART ① PETER ANDRE'S SO-CALLED LIFE QUIZ

So how intimate are you with Peter? Do you know all his secrets as well as the hard facts? See how many of the following 40 questions you can answer correctly...

1. WHERE WAS PETER BORN?
A) HARROW B) HASTINGS C) HARROGATE

2. WHAT DATE IN FEBRUARY IS PETER'S BIRTHDAY?
A) 14TH B) 29TH C) 27TH

3. AS A CHILD PETER WAS COMPARED TO ONE OF THE MUPPETS! BUT WHICH ONE?
A) FOZZIE BEAR B) KERMIT THE FROG C) GONZO

4. PETER'S CHILDHOOD TV HERO WAS...
A) THE SAINT B) DR WHO C) THE INCREDIBLE HULK

5. PETER'S A WATER SIGN BUT WHICH ONE...
A) SCORPIO B) PISCES C) CANCER

6. WHERE IN AUSTRALIA DID PETER LIVE?
A) AYERS ROCK B) GOLD COAST C) MELBOURNE

7. WHAT WAS THE NAME OF THE TALENT SHOW THAT BROUGHT PETER TO THE PUBLIC EYE IN AUSTRALIA?
A) NEW FACES B) STARS OF TOMORROW C) BIG TALENT

8. PETER'S RECORD COMPANY IS CALLED...
A) CAULIFLOWER B) TOMATO C) MUSHROOM

9. PETER'S FAVOURITE CHOCCY BAR IS...
A) DIME B) TOFFEE CRISP C) BOUNTY

10. WHICH OF PETER'S BROTHERS PLAYED GUITAR ON THE NATURAL TOUR?
A) DANNY B) CHRIS C) MICHAEL D) ANDREW

11. WHICH ACT HAS PETER ANDRE NEVER SUPPORTED?
A) BLACKSTREET B) MADONNA C) BACKSTREET BOYS

12. PETER'S MANAGEMENT COMPANY IS CALLED...
A) BLITZ B) CRASH C) SWIPE

13. PETER'S FAVOURITE FOOD IS...
A) THAI B) FRENCH C) MEXICAN

14. WHO IS PETER'S ULTIMATE PIN-UP?
A) TONI BRAXTON B) HALLE BERRY
C) NAOMI CAMPBELL

15. WHICH IS PETER'S FAVOURITE
EDDIE MURPHY MOVIE?
A) THE NUTTY PROFESSOR B) BEVERLY
HILLS COP C) COMING TO AMERICA

16. WHO DOES PETER SAY HE WOULD
MOST LIKE TO BE FOR THE DAY?
A) ALBERT EINSTEIN B) MICHAEL JACKSON
C) BRUCE LEE

17. WHAT TYPE OF SHEETS DOES PETER HAVE
ON HIS BED AT HOME?
A) TARTAN FLANNEL B) SPIDERMAN PRINT
C) BLACK SATIN

18. HOW MANY SIT-UPS DOES PETER
DO A DAY?
A) 1,000 B) 75 C) 300

19. WHICH *HOME & AWAY* ACTRESS DID PETER
ONCE DATE?
A) ISLA FISHER B) LAURA VASQUEZ
C) TEMPANY DECKERT

20. WHICH OF THESE THREE VIDEOS DID
PETER NOT SHOOT IN LA?
A) FLAVA B) NATURAL C) ONLY ONE

PART 2, ANSWERS AND SCORE, ON PAGE 57...

Photography by Guido Karp

ANATOMY OF PETER ANDRE

Listen to Peter's bodytalk...

HAIR

I've actually poked myself in the eye with these tendrils of hair! I've even eaten half of one once when I was eating some soup!

MIND

What is always on your mind?

I'm mostly focused on work and 80% of the time I'm very vibed and positive but there is a niggly negative voice in my head that is always asking me, What if...?

The other thing I do is wonder about other people's lives - I don't sit in a taxi and think, this bloke is paid to take me to the airport so get me there! I start thinking, this is probably his tenth job today, he could be sitting in the car thinking about going home to watch Hill Street Blues or what his wife's going to make for supper. I wonder what he feels when he goes home at night - whether he's glad it's all over or can't wait to get in the cab the next morning. Everyone's got a story and I'm always wondering what it might be!

HEAD

How do you feel about everyone presuming that you are big-headed?

I don't blame them at all but I'm really not like that. I think people are starting to realize because they see me interviewed on TV wearing jumpers and jackets rather than skimpy vests. It's the image that launched me but things change. I only had my shirt off for one number on the Natural Tour.

EARS

What whispered sweet nothing meant the most to you?

The best thing I can hear is someone complimenting me on my voice. That means so much to me. Bryan Adams once said I sounded like Smokey Robinson when I do ballads and that blew me away!

EYES

Are you a visual person?

Very much so, I have these visual ideas that would seem impossible in someone else's mind but I'm so sure that I can make it happen. I think if you put something so strong in your mind and believe that you will achieve it, you will at least get half way.

NOSE

How do you feel about people being so nosey about your private life?

I don't really mind because when people are taking that much interest in you it means you are a big success! And there is always somewhere in the world you can go where you won't be known. I have definitely used Eddie Murphy's line 'I am a goat herder' when people ask me what I do!

MOUTH

Kiss and tell!

A kiss always meant more to me than starting off the rest of the business. I remember I used to kiss this girl called Miranda and the kiss was so wonderful it seemed to go on for hours! I love lips, I love watching them move when a girl talks.

CHEEK
Do you turn the other cheek or fight back?
I was bullied a lot at school so I had to fight back but I was always more interested in protecting other people than starting any aggro. I've done boxing and kick-boxing so I can look after myself.

NECK
What do you get it in the neck for?
I used to get criticized for the amount of thank yous I would say in one evening! People thought I didn't mean it but it was the way we were brought up. Even now, I have these little moments where I think, everyone is working so hard to make me successful and I start getting all emotional and thanking everyone!
The thing my Dad told me not to say is 'sorry' because he would say, 'You're not sorry. If you were you wouldn't have done it in the first place.' And you know what? He's got a point!

SHOULDER
What is the biggest responsibility you feel rests on your shoulders?
Pleasing the people who come and see me do a live show. I'm such a perfectionist and it really bugs me if I walk off stage and I haven't given a good show because I feel the fans deserve more.

ARMS
Who do you wrap your arms around?
I get a feeling from holding my mum that satisfies me in such a natural way - hugging someone you care about just warms your heart. Sometimes that's all you need.

ELBOW
Do you get the elbow or give it?
A lot of times it's by mutual agreement, not necessarily

wanting to split up but agreeing it's the best thing to do. I know when they are thinking it but I'm usually the one that'll say it.

HANDS
Are you good with your hands?
I'd like to think so!

STOMACH
Apart from your six-pack, what else do you bring to a party?
The right state of mind!

HIPS
Where do you get those x-rated moves from?
There's this thing in kick-boxing called matrix that Jean-Claude Van Damme uses. You don't just stretch, you use every little muscle in your body so when it comes to dancing you are so flexible.

LEGS
Are you a leg man?
Well, I'm actually more likely to be noticing a girl's bottom! The other thing that really attracts me is her eyes and the way she looks at me.

HEART
Who has permanent residence in your heart?
There's a lot of people I get along with but very few that I click with. My family and my best friends always have a place in my heart.

KNEES
Who would you kneel before and say: I'm not worthy!
Music-wise I think Stevie Wonder is unbelievable.

FEET
Do feet make you cringe?
No, I know some people hate feet but I think a woman's toes are beautiful!

PLAY IT AGAIN, PETER!

BROTHER CHRIS - *Only One* - I just love the music to this one! It sounds great live.

MANAGEMENT CLAIRE - *I Feel You* - Peter recorded this in Copenhagen and when he first played it down the phone to me I thought it was one of the best songs I've ever heard!

CHOREOGRAPHER PAUL - *Natural* - the dancing and singing make a really powerful combination.

BROTHER DANNY - *Dream A Little* - Chris wrote the music, Peter wrote the lyrics. It hasn't been released here. That's my all-time favourite but I also like *Take Me Back, I Feel You* and *Mysterious Girl*.

MANAGEMENT SUE - *You Are* - A simple, yet beautiful ballad that will prove to be timeless.

PUBLICIST PETER - *Show U Something* - because it has a raunchy energy to it!

Here are the favourite Peter Andre songs of a dozen of his family and work colleagues...

Photography by Guido Karp

ANNUAL AUTHOR BELINDA - *Tell Me When* - because it's so smooth, it makes you drift off to a dreamy place! And I love the 'all night long' break in *Only One!*

TOUR MANAGER/PA NIGEL - *Message To My Girl* - because it has a timeless class to it.

BIG MAGAZINE'S FRAN - *Natural* - because it's such an uplifting song. I did a report from the video shoot in LA so every time I hear it, it reminds me of the good time I had!

FAN CLUB's MIKE - *Mysterious Girl* - because it is such perfect, bubblegum reggae pop! I think it's going to have a really long life - I can imagine an old pianist tinkling away in some Caribbean bar years from now. Probably with me dancing to it!

DANCER ZEUS - *Flava* - because I can dance to it freestyle, no problem!

BIRTH CHART

We had a birth chart drawn up without revealing the identity of the subject (Peter Andre of course!) and then assessed the most accurate statements!

RELATIONSHIPS

You are friendly, enjoy your social life and have a wide circle of friends, many of whom come from the world of music or a related area like public relations.
Peter gets along very well with the folk in the music business including performers like Robbie Williams, Backstreet Boys and Damage. At a recent London gig Eternal and Ant & Dec came along to see Peter perform.

Many of your friendships will be with the opposite sex.
Is it any wonder? He certainly has a way with women!

You're drawn to kind, easy-going people.
Rather like himself!

Friendship brings you many benefits including luck, protection and support.
To know Peter is to care about him and his friends would do anything for him.

Your social grace and willingness to mix with all types of people in a relaxed, open-minded way makes you popular.
Peter has an easy charm few can resist!

You are gentle in what you say, lending a sympathetic ear and leave certain things unsaid if you feel they will cause ill-feeling.
Peter is known for his wonderful manners. He's careful about what he says and would never knowingly hurt someone's feelings. He also gives the impression you could confide anything in him.

People find your magnetism very exciting.
He certainly has a presence, a star quality that gives the people around him a thrill.
His touchy feely approach to his fans gives them a real buzz.

Photography by Guido Karp

Sometimes you sense what
is on a person's mind.
Peter is very sensitive and aware of other
people's feelings.

You can pick up on other people's expressions or mannerisms.
His brothers always refer to his uncanny impressions of TV stars like the Incredible
Hulk. Maybe he could have been the next Rory Bremner if he hadn't got into music!

Your family exerts a great influence in your life.
Just look around him - he works with two of his brothers and speaks to his mum
several times a week, even though she's in Australia. He says his best friend is his
brother Michael.

Photography by Guido Karp

WORK

Your work needs to encompass a physical aspect.
Both in his work-outs and dancing on stage Peter is a physical guy!

A career in films could work.
There has been talk of Peter getting into movies so this sounds encouraging!

Once your ambitions have found a target you will work hard and systematically to reach it.
Peter's manager Claire says the great thing about Peter is that he will never, ever quit!

You have some very strong convictions and can persuade people with an air of confidence.
Manager Claire also says his success is due to the fact that he is so utterly involved in everything from the songwriting and image to video editing and fan club!

42 PETER PA ANDRE

Photography by Clair Powell

TALENTS

You have an excellent sense of rhythm - music and dance are good outlets for you.
Dance has always been a major part of Peter's performance, ever since he got a
couple of school friends to work on routines with him for lunch-time concerts!

With your strong imagination and inner ambition you have the ability to make
things that most people only dream about become a reality.
People always questioned Peter's absolute belief that he would make it but he never
wavered from his dream. He knew that if he put the effort in he would get a result.

You can become someone extraordinary yet remain sincere and humble.
One of the most common words people use to describe Peter is sincere! And despite
his heady level of success he remains wonderfully down-to-earth.

You'll get recognition for your acts of compassion.
Peter wrote the song *You Are* for a girl with a terminal illness. Despite his frantic
schedule he takes the time to respond to charity requests and he has reached out to
those who are suffering.

Your mind is more intuitive than strictly logical. Ideas come to you through
daydreams, feelings or on a psychic level (even if you are not always aware of it).
You express your thoughts through art or music or writing.
Peter gets inspiration at strange times - he's written several lyrics in the bath!

No doubt you have a sense of humour and can tell stories or jokes with funny
accents.
Peter cannot help but go into Eddie Murphy impressions and often talks in an Italian
accent, usually gangster style! His brother Chris says he finds silly things like Jim
Carrey movies incredibly funny and Peter always has some dodgy joke to share!

You are very sexual but manage to keep that aspect of you in good taste.
We can't argue with that!

QUESTIONS USING ALBUM • TRACKS AS INSPIRATION!

My favourite FLAVA is... coconut! But I'm also very partial to freshly squeezed mango juice!

I FEEL YOU - What is the sexiest texture? Satin! I love my black satin sheets!

I'm a NATURAL at... being crazy! Ever since I was a kid I've been doing impressions of Mafia men and Eddie Murphy!!

ALL I EVER WANTED was.... to be on stage performing! I got my wish!

The most MYSTERIOUS thing about GIRLs is... Where do I start?! (But I love them!) In a way *I Feel You* is about the confused feeling a woman can bring to you. It's one of those relationships where everything seems fine - when you see each other you can joke and talk serious. But something inside you feels it ain't right, something feels like they are playing you or that you are standing there like a fool and they are having the last laugh. I'd written about it because I knew people who had been through it but I'd never experienced it for myself. But how's this for something strange - I went through it word for word after I wrote it. Just two months later I was so down about this girl that I'd been crazy about I couldn't believe it.

TO THE TOP Apart from the charts, what else would you like to go to the top of? The Statue of Liberty!

SHOW U SOMETHING - what would you like to show the world? What I have to offer!

ONLY ONE... What your unique gift? I'm the 'only one' who can... claim writing royalties on Tell Me When!! I wrote the whole thing!

TURN IT UP What music do you like hearing at full volume? Keith Sweat - he's cool!

MESSAGE TO MY GIRL - Do you write love letters? I've only ever written one, it must have been bad because I didn't get one back! I think I'll stick to songs!

YOU ARE - What compliment do you get paid most often? People often tell me that I am happy! My dad always taught us to be positive and that's a great gift.

GET DOWN ON IT What is your idea of a great night out? Partying with friends - because you can do that anywhere!

TELL ME WHEN... you knew you were going to be a superstar... I sang I Just Called To Say I Love You by Stevie Wonder in a school band competition when I was a little kid. I remember standing backstage at Miami Great Hall on the Gold Coast of Australia - I was so nervous but I went out there and I tell you, I sang that song like I meant it. I looked into the crowd at the faces and I didn't know whether it sounded good or not but I knew that I was feeling that song. When I finished the crowd really responded and it was at that moment I realized I had to be a performer. It was also the day I got my first ever fan - there was this one girl up at the back of the hall and I never found out who she was or got a chance to say hello but she followed me from that day on.

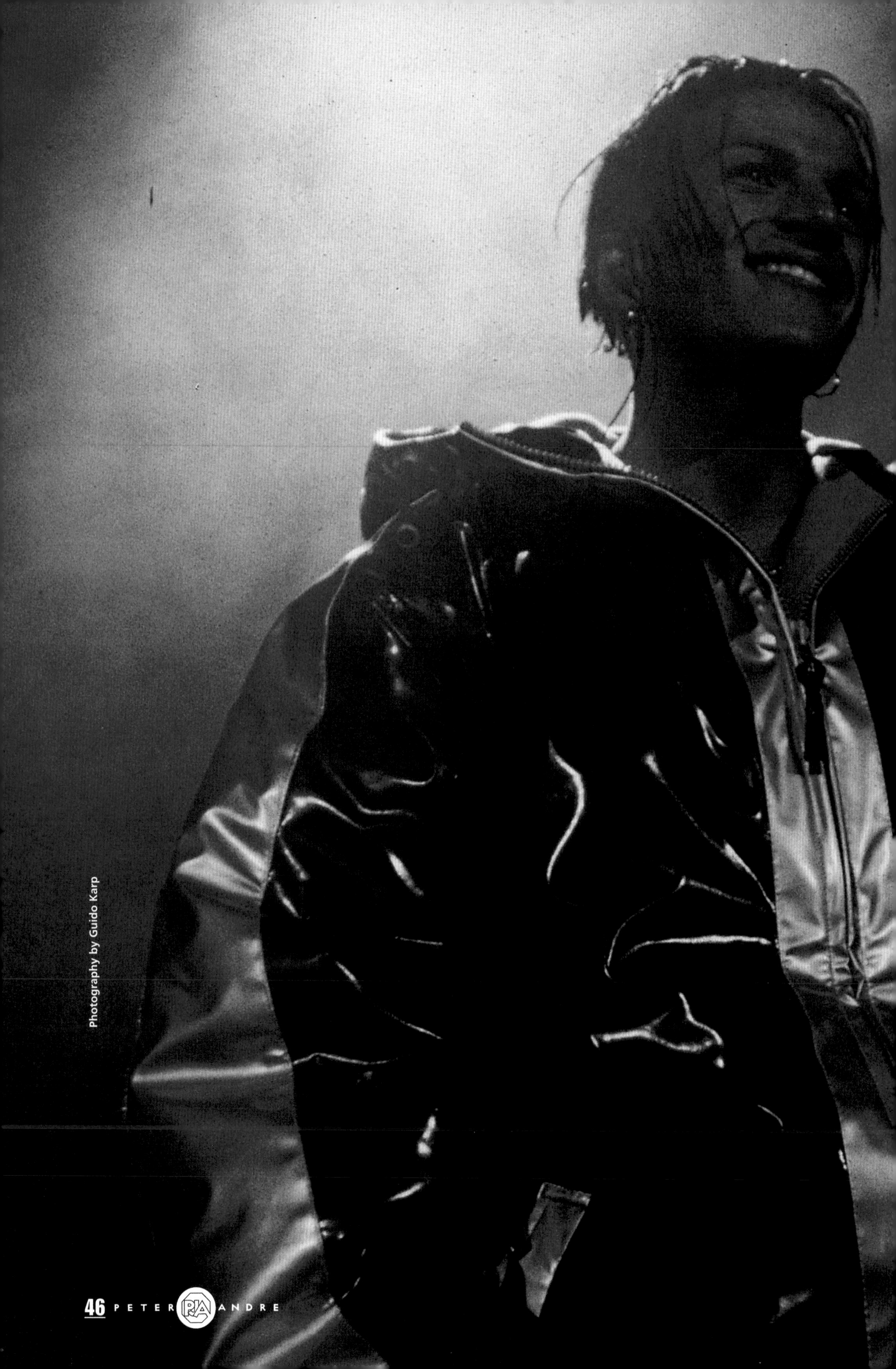

Photography by Guido Karp

IF I HAD THREE WISHES

What would you wish for?

1. No more hunger

2. No cruelty to animals - or to people

3. Wisdom of Einstein - when he was alive!

PETER'S
MUSIC COLLECTION

First record I bought
Off The Wall by Michael Jackson

Most recent CD I bought
The Blackstreet album

Most played track on my stereo
My, My, My by Johnny Gill

All-time favourite album
Motown Collection

Should have been a single from *Natural*
All I Ever Wanted (but remixed!)

I love singing
My Cherie Amour

I'm proudest of the vocal on
I Feel You

The song that gets me going
Show U Something (tour mix!)

Most emotional track
Lonely, off the new album

My sexiest lyric is from *I Feel You*: 'If only you'd come through the door, I
can't ignore, all of the loving you ever need and I wanna give you more'..

The real show-stopper on tour *Flava*

Favourite cover version I've done *Shake Your Body Down* by The Jackson

Cover version I want to do *Lady Love Me One More* Time by George Bens

Photography by Guido Karp

PETER ANDRE **49**

24 HOURS WITH PETER ANDRE

Here we look at one day out of Peter's heavy-duty schedule...

1.30pm	arrive at Midland Hotel, Manchester, for check-in, sign autographs in foyer, dump bags in room, make calls
3.15pm	arrive at Manchester Apollo, quick cuddle with freezing fans at stage door.
3.45pm	start vocal warm-up to 'open the throat' for sound check
4.00pm	interview for the official Peter Andre biography while eating late lunch of soup, fish and veggies.
5.00pm	sound check, problem with ear piece so this overruns...
5.45pm	press interviews with *Big* magazine and local press
6.30pm	meet and greet fans and competition winners
7.00pm	meeting with management
8.00pm	more vocal warm-up for performance
8.20pm	sit-ups and press-ups
8.40pm	get into first outfit
9.00pm	burst onto stage
10.30pm	hurry onto tour bus before fans spill out of venue

Photography by Guido Karp

10.45pm   back to hotel to shower and change

11.45pm   travel to new restaurant opening late for a private party for Peter, cast members of Coronation St and Hollyoaks attend.

12 midnight   signing autographs for diners at restaurant, including one plaster cast!

1.00am   finally sit down to meal, chatting to journalists, support acts, publicity

2.30am   back to hotel bar, great atmosphere - no-one wants to go to bed

5.30am   finally give in and head back to room to sleep before 11am wake-up call

12 midday   check-out of hotel and climb aboard the tour bus for the 4-hour journey to the next venue where it will start all over again!

SAY ANYTHING!

Here are our Top Ten favourite tongue twisters from Peter Andre!

1. Me and mirrors don't get along!

2. I can't quite get to grips with the way it's exploded for me - it's like there was a gap there for me!

3. Sometimes I can get a bit jealous because I like the girl to be mine and just mine and likewise I'll be hers and just hers.

4. I am a perfectionist. But it's not that I want to be perfect - I just want everything I do to be as perfect as I can make it.

5. When I was young I thought people would laugh at me wanting to be a singer so I said I was going to be an architect!

6. I have a lot of days when I think, 'What is it that people see in me?' And then other days I feel good and I think, 'I'm going to show them what I've got!'

7. I'm the biggest flirt I know!

8. It's just as annoying for me to have hair like this as it is for people to look at!

9. I'm soft but I can also be quite an animal!

10. Sometimes I feel like the only kid who bought the Willy Wonka chocolate bar with the winning ticket!

JOIN OUR CLUB!

IF YOU WANT UP-TO-DATE INFORMATION ON PETER
YOU MAY LIKE TO JOIN HIS CLUB...

ADDRESS
PETER ANDRE FANCLUB, PO BOX 236, Stanmore, Middlesex HA7 2UF

YOU WILL RECEIVE:
A full-colour poster
Four A5 glossy colour photos
A flexi-plastic membership card bearing your personal number
A metal lapel photo badge
A Peter Andre Fan Club pen
The current Peter Andre Talks Back Cassette - recorded exclusively for members

COST: £11

FAN CLUB FACTS
The average age of the fan club member - 16. But of course there are also a large number of pre-teens and older teens who love him too.

The fan club was launched - November 1996

The number of fan club members - 8,000 and growing!

The number of fans who send photos of themselves - under 10%

The most-asked question - Can I have a backstage pass?

The most unusual request - a fan wanted Peter to sign a pair of knickers.

The most unusual invitation - one girl sent a video of her parents B&B hotel near the venue of one of Peter's gigs and invited him to stay there.

The most given gift - cuddly toys.

The most unusual gift - a beautiful oil painting a fan did of Peter.

The most letters sent - one girl has written every week, the fan club gets several hundred letters a day.

Mike Hrano of The Peter Andre Fan Club says: 'When it comes to his fan club Peter is an extremely professional, ambitious guy. He wants it to be the biggest and the best! He's very switched on and pays painstaking attention to what I do on his behalf - getting actively involved and scrutinizing and approving everything. He takes a genuine, sincere interest in his fans and really appreciates the fact that he is where he is today because of them. Peter is very approachable but he also has a certain mystique about him and when you see him perform live you know that he was born to do this. He is a complete star!'

PART ②
PETER ANDRE'S
SO-CALLED LIFE QUIZ

21. WHICH ACTION HERO DOES PETER MOST ADMIRE?
A) ARNIE SCHWARZENEGGER B) JEAN-CLAUDE VAN DAMME C) SYLVESTER STALLONE

22. WHICH MTV SHOW DID PETER PRESENT?
A) STYLISSIMO B) MOST WANTED C) SELECT

23. WHICH SONG WAS PETER'S FIRST UK NUMBER 1?
A) *MYSTERIOUS GIRL* B) *FLAVA* C) *I FEEL YOU*

24. WHAT IS PETER'S IDEA OF A GREAT HOLIDAY?
A) BEACHBUMMING IN BARBADOS B) SKIING IN THE FRENCH ALPS C) CITY SIGHTS IN NEW YORK

25. WHAT WAS THE NAME OF PETER'S FIRST LOVE?
A) MELISSA B) MELANIE C) MIRANDA

26. WHICH TV SHOW HAS PETER *NOT* GUEST PRESENTED?
A) *BIG BREAKFAST* B) *THE CLOTHES SHOW* C) *TOP OF THE POPS*

27. WHICH IS PETER'S FAVOURITE PERFUME ON A WOMAN?
A) *CK ONE* BY CALVIN KLEIN B) *KNOWING* BY ESTEE LAUDER C) *ENVY* BY GUCCI

28. PETER ONCE HAD A CAT NAMED AFTER A FRENCH CITY, BUT WHICH ONE?
A) LYON B) CALAIS C) PARIS

29. PETER'S LONG-TERM GIRLFRIEND KATHY MODELLED FOR WHICH FASHION HOUSE?
A) CHANEL B) YVES SAINT LAURENT C) GIVENCHY

30. WHAT DOES PETER WEAR TO BED?
A) BOXER SHORTS B) PYJAMA BOTTOMS C) NOTHING

31. WHEN PETER WAS YOUNG HE WISHED HIS NAME WAS
A) JEROME B) JAKE C) JEREMY

32. WHAT WAS PETER'S FATHER'S PROFESSION?
A) HAIRDRESSER B) TAILOR C) OPERA SINGER

33. WHICH COUNTRY WAS THE *MYSTERIOUS GIRL* VIDEO SHOT IN ?
A) MALAYSIA B) THAILAND C) INDIA

34. WHICH OF PETER'S *NATURAL TOUR* DANCERS HAS BEEN WITH HIM THE LONGEST?
A) SLY B) VALERIE C) ZEUS D) PAULETTE

35. WHAT IS PETER'S MIDDLE NAME?
A) JAMES B) JOE C) JEFFREY

36. WHAT PIECE OF JEWELLERY IS ALWAYS AROUND PETER'S NECK?
A) IVORY PENDANT ON A LEATHER STRIP B) PJA INITIALS IN SILVER C) GOLD CHAIN

37. WHAT COLOUR IS PETER'S JEEP IN THE *FLAVA* VIDEO?
A) ELECTRIC BLUE B) SHIMMERY SILVER C) JET BLACK

38. WHAT DOES PETER USE TO MOISTURIZE HIS SKIN?
A) BABY OIL B) COCOA BUTTER C) GOLDEN SYRUP

39. WHAT WAS THE BACKDROP FOR THE *NATURAL* VIDEO?
A) A GOLF COURSE B) A SKI RESORT C) AN AIRPORT

40. WHICH LONDON VENUE DOES PETER DREAM OF PLAYING ONE DAY?
A) WEMBLEY STADIUM B) HOUSE OF COMMONS C) ROYAL ALBERT HALL

ANSWERS

1. A) HARROW - AT NORTHWICK PARK HOSPITAL
2. C) 27TH FEBRUARY - 1973
3. B) JENNY - BECAUSE OF HIS CUTE DIMPLES
4. C) THE INCREDIBLE HULK
5. B) YES
6. B) GOLD COAST - SURFER'S PARADISE
7. A) NEW FACES
8. C) MUSHROOM
9. B) TOFFEE CRISP - HE'S ALSO VERY PARTIAL TO CADBURY'S SPONGE MINI ROLLS!
10. B) CHRIS - DANNY DOES THE 'BEAUTY'
11. A) BLACKSTREET
12. A) BLITZ - HIS MANAGERS' NAMES ARE CLAIRE AND SUE
13. A) THAI - ESPECIALLY THE CHICKEN DISHES
14. B) HALLE BERRY WITH TONI BRAXTON - A CLOSE RIVAL!
15. C) COMING TO AMERICA - PETER LOVES THE 'PEANUTS' SCENE
16. A) EINSTEIN - 'JUST TO EXPERIENCE THAT WISDOM'.
17. C) BLACK SATIN
18. C) 300
19. B) LAURA VASQUEZ
20. C) ONLY ONE - FILMED IN AUSTRALIA
21. B) JEAN-CLAUDE VAN DAMME
22. A) STYLISSIMO
23. B) FLAVA
24. A) BEACHBUMMING IN BARBADOS
25. C) MIRANDA
26. B) THE CLOTHES SHOW
27. B) KNOWING BY ESTEE LAUDER - MY GIRLFRIEND WORE IT AND I WILL LOVE IT FOR EVER SINCE!
28. C) PARIS
29. B) YVES SAINT LAURENT
30. C) NOTHING!
31. A) JEROME - 'AFTER A CARTOON CHARACTER WHO HAD TWO EARRINGS AND WORE HIS CAP BACK-TO-FRONT, I REALLY WANTED TO BE LIKE HIM!'
32. A) + B) HAIRDRESSER & TAILOR!
33. B) THAILAND
34. C) ZEUS
35. A) JAMES
36. C) GOLD CHAIN
37. A) ELECTRIC BLUE
38. B) COCOA BUTTER
39. C) AIRPORT
40. A) WEMBLEY STADIUM - HE PLAYED THE ROYAL ALBERT HALL IN MARCH THIS YEAR!

SCORES

1-10 'ONLY ONE' TO TEN? TSK! A PENALTY OF 500 SIT-UPS IMMEDIATELY!

10-20 YOU'RE GETTING THERE. YOU JUST NEED TO 'TURN IT UP' A BIT! PERHAPS IF YOU COULD TEAR YOUR EYES AWAY FROM HIS STOMACH FOR ONE MINUTE...!

20-30 YOU MAY NOT HAVE ALL THE ANSWERS BUT YOU HAVE CERTAINLY GOT THE 'FLAVA' OF PETER ANDRE. FEEL FREE TO THROW YOUR HANDS UP IN THE AIR!

30-40 YOU'RE A 'NATURAL'! IN FACT YOU KNOW SO MUCH ABOUT HIM WE SUSPECT YOU MAY SECRETLY BE HIS GIRLFRIEND! CONFESS!

Photography by Guido Karp

INTO THE FUTURE

Peter has got big plans for the future - he wants to make this thing last well into the millenium!

LOOKS

I'm going to go for a more clean-cut, classy look. I'm not going to cover up completely but I'll focus on a different part of my body than my stomach! And yes, I am going to get my hair cut!

SONGS

I've always longed to work with American producers like Babyface and just recently I had the incredible experience of meeting with Rod Templeton who is the guy who wrote Thriller for Michael Jackson. It was such an honour to talk with him and I would love to work with him in the future.

Personally I've always been more R&B/soul/swing-orientated than pop-orientated so I can see myself going more in that direction. For the next album I want to move up a level but still keep the flow. If you jump into something totally new it just slaps the fans in the face. I don't want to do that because the fans are the reason I am here.

TOURS

My dream is touring arenas around the world. I love performing on stage, it's what I do best! I'd love one day to know that I could fill Wembley Stadium - that would be the ultimate wow! It's going to be years in the making but hey, I'm going for it!

MOVIES

A few projects are being discussed at the moment... I'd love to follow in the action comedy footsteps of Eddie Murphy and Wil Smith - I love the combination of hard physical and crazy humour!

GIRLS

I'm still looking for the real girl for me and I hope I'll find her in the not-too-distant future! It can be fun being single but I think you are only truly content when you have someone to love. It fills that gap in your life.

HOMES

My ideal home would have it's own leisure centre with a swimming pool, steam room and jacuzzi and an aquarium built into the whole of one wall! A place that can be as romantic or as fun as you want it to be.

My family is based in Australia but I have a home in London and I'd like a second home in America - I saw the houses in Bel Air in Los Angeles and fell in love! I'd like one day to buy a house there - I love the summer life, sitting out on the veranda with a long, cool drink... That would be bliss!

See you in the year 2000!

DISCOGRAPHY

UK

SINGLE	RELEASED	HIGHEST CHART POSITION
Turn It Up	June 95	64
Mysterious Girl	September 95	53
Only One	March 96	16
Mysterious Girl	May 96	2
Flava	September 96	1
I Feel You	November 96	1
Natural	February 97	6

ALBUM

Natural	September 96	1